Conversations with Mr. Hooker Volume One

Let's talk Bars first as there are always fun things happening in the bars. Then in chapter two let's talk about romance, women and a few broken heart stories thrown in for balance.

Volume 2 will focus more on friends and family, nature and God. Coming in July, 2017

Chapter One
Bar Poems and Lyrics

Over the Shoulder Love
He's sitting at the bar the glass is not to far
Over his shoulder he glances at her
Not too long, don't want to get caught
He sees her smile, sees her flip her hair
He's sitting at the bar the glass is not to far
Over his shoulder he glances at her
She sees the glance and smiles in his direction
He's been caught and turns away
He's sitting at the bar his glass is not to far
I ask why not go talk to her
I talk to her and it goes bad he said
I can never glance at her again
He's sitting at the bar the glass is not to far

End or beginning
I am talking to a friend and I see her
across the room
The smile, the sparkle in her eye, I glance
away
I look again, did she see me looking, I
glance away
I look again she is looking at me, I smile at
her
Will she smile at me
Will she take the risk of showing her
interest
If so she will be mine one day

Night shift
The crack of the Q ball
The buzz of the bulls' eye
The music is playing
The laugh and the flirt are here
Night has fallen in the bar
Food food food
Everyone wants food
Shots shots shots
Everyone wants shots
More shots shots shots
Q ball is stuck in the table
Can I get change for the tables
Last call
Shots shots shots
More shots
Closing time don't have to go home
Just can't stay here
Oh thank God night shift is over

Repeat over and over and over
I work
I sit in my room
I sleep
I work
I sit in my room
I sleep
I work
I get paid
I drink
I sleep
In jail

Karaoke
Singing out loud
Singing to myself
Singing to them
No one cares how bad I sing
No one cares if I sing
But it is my time to sing
And sing I will
I'll sing the country
I'll sing the pop
I'll sing no rock
Everyone is gone
But time for one more song
And sing I will

DUI #3
I'm a little tipsy the room did a flip
I'm a little tipsy think I'll be sick
I'm a little tipsy let's take a trip
I'm a little tipsy….sorry officer

Running down the road
Running down the road just as fast as I can
Running down the road just ahead the law
Running down the road just as naked as can be
Running down the road just trying to find my clothes
Running down the road in the back of the police car
Running down the road no more

Streaker
Who's that naked man running across the room
Who's that naked man running out the door
Who's that naked man in my bar.
Streaker running in my bar
I will remember you man I will remember you

Here
Can't smoke here
Can toke but not here
Can drink here
Can't get drunk here
Can flirt here
Can't touch here
Can laugh here
Cant laugh loud here
Can play here
Can't win here
Can sing here only when it's your turn

Becky
I had sat at the bar
Sat across from the woman we all loved
I loved her, only from afar
She loved another she moved away far
She died alone on a highway
I cried for so long for she was dead long ago
What if I had stolen her heart?
What if I made her love me
What if I had made love to her
We would never have parted
Stood together
But she loved another she moved far away
She died alone on a highway

USA! USA! USA!
He fought in the war, I bought him a beer
His hands shook, his chest racked
 His voice so soft, his eyes so angry
 My guilt fills my heart with sadness
But pity is not his desire to quench his fire
Nor justice or vindication
What was the cause he chokes, to protect us?
What would victory have achieved?
Who will live better a thousand years from now?
For the lives that I took in war, for the friends lost
We both know, no greatness was to be achieved
Only the glory and profit of our masters
For slaves we are and slaves we will be
Till tomorrow and let the warriors lead the way
He fought in the war he died in his sleep
Lead the way my warrior lead the way

Free spirit
She moves to her own beat
Across the dance floor
The music follows her
The smile is a treat for us all
Her hair like silk in the wind
The room is hers
But who has her heart
Only she knows
Will she ever tell?
Only she knows

Really!
So I was sitting outside one night
Having a smoke, can't smoke in the bar
She sat beside me with no introduction
Started to tell me about her life
I had another smoke, can't smoke in the bar
I asked her name and she told me her tits were real
I asked her name again and she showed me her tits
They were real, and I still can't smoke in the bar

Good morning
I unlock the door and run to the alarm
The smell is always the same
Old beer, old smoke, old sweat
The spills are always in the same places
The chairs a mess, the tables dirty
The bathrooms strewn with debris and stink
The kitchen smells of fried food
Behind the bar is sticky with alcohol and fruit
Out front the cigarette butts abound
The ash tray is over flowing
Tell me again why I loved this place so

When a ten was not enough
Before I could see her face
Her laughter filled the room
Before I could see her face
Her eyes shone out of the crowd as if in the moonlight
Before I could see her face
Her smile lit up the room
Before I could see her face
Her voice filled the room as a gentle wind in the trees
When I did see her face
My world changed
After I had seen her face
I never saw another

Enough
I heard something, a pop
Was it a shot
Was it a pop
I looked outside
A man pointed a long gun at me
Go inside sir
So I did
Time to get the fuck out of here

Drive responsibly
The jager bombs fell like bombs over Iraq
The jager shots came like wasps from a disturbed nest
No driving home tonight
Walking it
Each step goes past
Have to focus on the next
Don't fall don't fall don't fall
Oh shit I fell, back up we go
Don't fall don't fall don't fall
Don't get to close to the road
Don't fall don't fall don't fall
Where did that sign post come from
Don't fall don't fall don't fall
The porch the knob
Oh crap the key
In
Ok to fall now

Easy street
The day is ending
The sun is setting
I stand outside smoking
I am tired and weary
But my day is only half over
For the money time is yet to come
Hopefully it will come
May this be a worthy day
I pray to myself
What I give today will cost me two days at the end
I'd give three days for it to be a worthy day

Liven the dream
My brother my brother
I am here to wonder
What new adventures have you had
What new adventures you plan
My day is plain and hard with labor
And yours filled with wonder and ventures
Aye to own a bar the thing to dream
My day is filled with wonder
The wonder of how my customers are so sad
The wonder of their anger and resentment to life
The wonder of how they endure the pain in their lives
The wonder of how they live still
Yes live they do and so I wonder
The American dream is a lie and a cheat
Only the rich get rich
And the one per cent prospers
The rest of us but are here to be robbed
Then put out in the street when we are old
But for today I live the dream

Thursday night
The warriors arrive in ones and pairs seldom more
More than a hundred will they number
They gather their equipment, test the fit and function
Clean and polish for today it is do or die
They banter back and forth soon they will know who is friend and foe
The battle will be bloody and there will be those not seen again
Tempers will lose a battle, calm will the victors be
The finial victor will be weary, covered with blood and sweat
But the victory will be clear no doubt who won
A man turns to me in wonder and asks what goes here
Foosball my friend Foosball

The day has just begun but the day is done
The day has just begun but the day is done
Its 2am and we close the till
Put up the chairs
Sweep the floors
Wipe the bar
The day has just begun but the day is done
Who slumbers after a shift
The night has just begun for all those servers
The night has just begun for all those bartenders
The day has just begun but the day is done
Oh the house parties
The casinos with slots and pull tabs
It is play time for those who labor so late into the night
The love affairs, the drunken antics that will be tomorrow's lore
 All this while the sheep slumber
And as your alarm goes off they will begin to nod off
The day has just begun but the day is done

Bartenders Song
Fucking idiot
Fucking idiot
Fucking idiot
Fucking idiot
There now let's try again shall we
What can I get you
Rum with no coke or fruit
A whiskey with no soda or water
But you can't decide on anything here
A beer no one has heard of before
A wine we don't carry
Here try this
What is it
A fucking drink you asshole
Next

The Garfield/ River crossing
When I was younger
 There was this beer hall
That shared a parking lot
 With a Chinese's restaurant
With a full bar
So we rolled in to Garfield's first to get a pool table
Hung with who there
 Shot a game had a beer
 or two
Crossed the parking lot with a joint
Or two
Hung with who there
Played pull tabs
 Had a hard pop
Or two
Crossed the parking lot with a joint
Or two
Hung with who there
Shot a game, had a beer
Or two
When I was younger life was a lot less
Complicated

Neighborhood bar
He rolls in as smooth as honey on a hot day
Normally I toss the drug dealers
But he deals no street drugs he deals to the dealers
This is his social bar
He' cool I'm cool, we are all cool
They roll in like muddy water in a flood
The ride up on their bikes
But the colors and guns stay in the bags
This is their social bar
They cool, I'm cool, we are all cool
They roll in like the rap they will soon be playing on the juke
They wear their pants to their knees and their boxers over their naval.
They know the rules, no colors no guns, no problems
This is their social bar
They cool, I'm cool we all cool
They roll in like tumble weeds on a high wind
They all know the rules
Must have US ids to be in the bar
This is their social bar
They cool, I'm cool we all cool
Welcome to the neighborhood bar
In a working class neighborhood

Burning River
Oh shit the Rivers on fire
Crap I just ordered a beer
Now the cops are coming
Closing is in 15 minutes
Got to run got to run
Go before the cops get here
O shit the River is on fire
Slam my beer
Head for the door
Go before the cops get here
As I swing into my truck
I her the bartender ask
Did anyone call 911
Oh fuck it
I'm having another beer
Let the River burn
There are Chinese restaurants all over this town

The big cranes
Ray was big man
Who swung the big cranes
He called the radio stations
And reported on the city daily
Ray was a big drinker
Who swung the big cranes
He climbed the latter's
So high into the sky he looked down on the clouds
Ray lost his job when Bush depressed America
He no longer swung the big cranes
He no longer called the radio stations
He no longer looked down on the clouds
Ray was still a big drinker
Ray no longer swung the big cranes
Ray no longer swings any cranes
God rest you Ray

I just heard that Eddie Spaghetti has had to fight for his life against cancer. There are fund raising pages up but I don't know
if he is still with us or not.
But if you are Eddie here is a shout out from the old Tobys
If your still with us keep fighting and if you had to go, then we'll see you soon

Eddie Spaghetti
Eddie stood 6 foot 6 ish
Maybe an inch more
Maybe and inch lower
A beard longer than any I ever had
And I had some good beards
He and his band rocked where ever they played
Old dead and byrds tunes were a staple
Oh but you want to see a big man light up
When he played his music the rock was on
No one touched a dial yet the volume blew up
That guitar took on the life of Eddie Spaghetti
The house was entertained
Now it's alive
People were dancing
Now they are grooving
God bless you Eddie Spaghetti
And all that band
Where ever you are today Eddie
Rock the fuck out of it
Love ya man!!!

Big Shot
When you think you are the shit
You probably are a piece of shit
If you think your shit don't stink
You're probably breathing through your mouth
If you think your shits pretty
You fucked up man
I mean really fucked up
Man you need some major head shit brother
Or glasses

The old River
Sitting in the River drinking a scotch
Watching the boys looking for a notch
Bad boys in here they like to fight
Bad boys in here be here all night
Unless they get in a fight
Then the go low
Be away from the law
Bad boys looking for a fight
Won't be with me
That's been tried
Didn't work out so well
For the bad boys in the River
Now we just nod
Bad boys in the River
Bad boys looking for a fight

Backroom bars
Once was a broom closet now a bar
Place is always full and one in every hood
Along every old highway
No wonder it's always full it only seats seven.
The back bar a half dozen bottles most brown
Some clear and no fancy bottles.
Most of the time they are in Chinese places
Or old cafes along the highway
Locals are all known there
Strangers stick out like soy burgers at a barbeque
Most don't bother to speak to them
Unless they're pretty

Not so dumb
She was the sweetest girl in the bar
She was the prettiest girl in the bar
She was not the smartest girl in the bar
She would ask for a vodka lemon
Then ask what was in the drink
But we loved her and we took care of her
Made sure no one took advantage of her
Until one night she met her love
He got the sweetest girl in the bar
And the prettiest girl in the bar
But she was smarter than we thought
He was rich

Rats on floor
Late at night they broke a hole into my wall
They crawled like little rats to the back office
They stole the safe not so safe at all
But a mistake was made when the rat lifted his head
Snap snap the baby camera went snap snap
The rat turned to see what snapped and it was his picture
The rat was doomed from that day on
The news showed that rat's image all over town
The internet showed the rat's image to all who cared
All to no avail till rat himself bragged to a snitch
The picture on TV and the internet is mine said the rat
They want to make me famous
The rat was caught the rat was jailed
At least for a spell
Snap snap you little fucker I hope they snap you neck

Good Lord she was a looker
Good Lord she was a looker
That dress, so tight that she could not have carried a dime
If there had been a pocket.
Short and low cut was all that was needed
To bring the entire bar to a complete halt
No pool players played
The darts were held in mid air never leaving the fingers
The Foosball players hard core they all
Simply stared and allowed the ball to fall
Her hair looked like the wind was blowing it
While she was inside
He eyes so defiant and fiery
This was no bimbo
This was as deadly of a being as you will find
Nails that looked like they were made of stone
Not an ounce of fat on that body
No fear no fate for her she makes her way in this world
She never spoke a word
Her date ordered shots and they slammed them at the bar
He went to the restroom she looked only at me
Oh the smile
 I considered for a moment
What if I just left and never came back
 Good Lord she was a looker
Wish I had left with her
No matter what my life would have been better

Should have just stayed at the bar
Oh man rejection is a bitch
You say hello
They say hello you think ok
Now to actually start a conversation
Something a little clever but
Don't overdo it
Something cute but not to cute
Don't want to sound to eager
Hey baby nice …shoes…nice phone
Now don't wait for a response
Just run from the bar
Never go back there again
But no you are stuck
Can't run can't hide just take it
Blah blah blah blah
Slink back to your seat
Finish your drink
And get the hell out of there

George
They called him the Colonel
I called him George
He looked like a colonel
With the military walk
The square manly face
Look you straight in eye
Ask you a question
Tell you if he didn't like the answer
Some thought him loony
He was a bit off and had his demons
A child he didn't know well, maybe not at all
A life time in the Army seeing what others did not
He knew people
You could see the wariness in his eyes
When around those he did not know or trust
And if he did not like you the quiet was heavy in the air
But boy could he tell a story
I don't think the man every forgot a detail in his life
And don't rush him or he would just leave the table
George got sick and died many years ago
But every veteran's day George is who I picture in my mind
When I think of a soldier, an officer, a Colonel
Love you George see you soon

The Walking Lady
She was a loon plain and simple
We called her the walking lady
She came in the bar to drink her tea
Anyone talked to her she treated them like unwanted suitors
She walked for miles every day and went no where
She was known by many and knew no one
She was pretty in plain way
One summer day on the street above the bar
A car driven by a teen lost control and jumped the curb
There she walked on her journey to nowhere
She was killed instantly they said
Atlas she found some place to go
God bless you walking lady we miss you

Whatever happened to those four old guys
Every Monday, Tuesday and Friday they meet in the bar
Drink some beer play some pull tabs
Hanging with the big dogs they call it
Used to be they could smoke in the bar
Used to be there were four now there are three
Every Monday, Tuesday and Friday they meet in the bar
Drink some beer play some pull tabs
Hanging with the big dogs they call it
But one of the dogs is too sick to come anymore
Used to be there were four now there are two
Every Monday, Tuesday and Friday they meet in the bar
Drink some beer play some pull tabs
Hanging with the big dogs they call it
But today only one dog showed up
Used to be there were four now there is one
Every Monday, Tuesday and Friday he comes into the bar
Drinks some beer and plays some pull tabs
Hanging with the big dog he would call it if he spoke
He just sits quietly at the bar now
Used to be four, today no one showed up

Chapter two
Let's talk love, love lost, cute girls and what else comes to mind as go along in this chapter.

Can't talk love without a divorce or two or three of four. Oh crap!

Divorce

I'm awake but where am I
What time is it
Where is my wife
Where are my dogs
Who am I
Why am I here
Where is here
Why am I not in my bed
What did I do wrong
Oh lord not again

Love
I don't know where it started
I don't know where it ended
I just know I miss it sooooo

I don't give crap
I don't care no more
I don't care if you don't care
I don't care if you do care
I don't care no more
I don't give a shit what you think
I don't give a shit what you do
I don't give a shit
I don't think of you no more
I don't think of you at all
I don't think anymore
I don't know no more
I don't know how sad I am

Forever
Don't want to talk to you
Don't want to talk to no one
Don't want to see you
Don't want to see no one
I hurt I am in pain
Just leave me alone for fucking while
I'll get back just don't leave me now
Oh shit
She left me now
Got to find my way back
Got to dig out of this shit
There ahead is a light
Run for the light
Pull yourself up into the light
I can talk to you now
I'd like to see you now
But you left when the going got tough
Not like I did when you needed tough
It's ok
Better without you
You failed the test of love
And you will fail
Over and over again
And never understand that
Love is forever or not all

Why do I get so angry
Why do I get so angry
When I think of you
Why do I get so angry
When you do well
Why do I get so angry
When you talk
Why do I get so angry
When you walk
Why do I get so angry
When you are gone
Why do I get so angry
When you are home
So you want a divorce
Wow I feel so much better now
Thank you

Wait!!!
Waiting is the worst
Waiting in line is a bitch
Waiting at the ferry makes me twitch
Waiting for the doctor
Or worse yet waiting for the dentist
Everyone says make the most of this
But waiting to pay does not make my day
Waiting for someone else is terrible
Waiting to see if she will call
Or never be heard from again
Waiting makes me crazy makes my brain hazy
Will the phone ring or will this go on tomorrow
When will the waiting end
Hopefully just around the bend
The end
Oh but wait!

Run away with me

Do you want to run away with me?
Please oh please tell me yes
I so want to run away with someone
So let's runaway with you
Let's run away to some place warm
Let's run away to someplace no one knows us
Please lets run fast and far
We can worry about the details later
My name Don by the way
See one detail out of the way
I not worried about your name
Baby will do for now
You're so cute and so sexy what name do you want
I hope you have the money as I am too poor to care
Let's just get out of here

What do I remember?
The first time I seen her she passed by my door
The smile
The first time I heard her
The laugh
The first time we danced
Her happiness
The first time she made me happy
She kissed my cheek
The first time she discussed her family
Her joy
The first secrets told
We cried
The first time we made love
I belong to her forever

Diversion
I see the girl in the car next to us on the freeway
She is young, she's cute she's Asian she is on her phone
I see the Stater pulling up on her, she's on her phone still
She does not see the Stater when he lights her up
This bodes bad for the Asian hotie
The Stater bull horns to pull over, she is unhappy
I turn to my brother and say speed up the staters occupied

Pretty girls
Out for a walk
See a pretty girl walking
Good to see a pretty girl walking
Or what's the point of going for a walk
Out for a drive
See a pretty girl in the car next to you
Good thing to see a pretty girl out for a drive
Or what's the point of taking a drive
Sitting in a bar having a drink
See a pretty girl in the bar
Good to see a pretty girl in the bar
Or what's the point of going out to a bar
Pretty girls everywhere we go
Good that pretty girls are everywhere we go
Or what's the point of going anywhere

Profile
She looks for the man who will understand her
He must not be mean but be firm
Not a smoker, drinker of excess or 420 friendly
She rides a motorcycle, and wears leathers
She wants a man fit to do things with her
No couch potatoes she says
A man of means and faith in God
She jumps from planes, lines and cliffs
Love to kiss, not interested in hooking up
She wants to travel far away, is close to family
She wants to be dependant but independent too
She wants that special man
Damn right he has to be special
Motherfucker has be Christian biker head shrinker
To satisfy this nut case of a bitch

When two people
It's not what one person feels
That matters
It's when two people feel
You have the beginning of something
When two people talk on the phone
It's not a big deal
When two people talk on the phone
And it is a big deal for them both
It is a big deal
When two people embrace
The world goes on
It happens every day
When two people embrace
And the world stops moving
It should be happening every day
When two people make love
They are soon back to their lives
This happens every day
When two people make love
No one sees them again till the next day
This does not happen every day
When two people grow old together
All who know them
Prosper from the richness of that love

Someone not like any before
I seek I seek I want a true companion
Someone who is my champion
Someone who does not need to be rescued
From the clutches of the world or x husband
Someone secure in who they are today
Someone secure enough to not worry about what I do
Just that I am happy and treat them like a queen
Someone who will laugh with me till the end
Someone not trying to take something from anyone
Someone with love in their heart for the good in people
I can go anywhere now days
Arizona, Hawaii, Victoria, or California
A truck load of stuff is mine and my little dogs
And we can be off to anywhere
Preferably somewhere warm and nice and blue
Some place where the golf courses are fast
And traffic slow
Oh Lord let me be loved true by a real person

Hope
You came out of no where
Suddenly you were there
In a white dress, on a sunny day
I fell in love
I talked to you for weeks on end
Nary a word did you say
No stories no dreams no desires
Then one day I said enough
Tell me your dreams
Tell me your desires
Tell me you could love me
But you would not
I stopped telling you of my dreams
My fears
My stories
You would look through my door
On occasion
But still no words of love or hate
Then one day you were gone
No sign before no signal that you were leaving
Just off into the wind as if you had never existed
It would have been nice if you had said good bye
Given me a story something to remember you by
Now that spot in my heart is just vacant
A dim memory a fading picture
Of you in a white dress on a sunny day

Not lost
I wonder the fields of barley
I know where I started
I know not where I finish
I know not who I seek
I know not where you are
 I wonder the fields of barley
I would call your name
But I know it not it
Do you know I am seeking you

She never saw this poem
Her hair flowed like golden rich malt from a decanter
Her body flowed like a dancer mid performance
 She carried the flowers with a sense of joy
Only a gift from a lover would illicit such joy
The smile she beamed as she approached her date
That smile caused us all there who witnessed this act
To say to themselves oh but oh but me to be the one
To have sent those flowers
To have received that smile

My three wishes
She had eyes of blue
Hair of honey
A hint of her smile
Was all she needed
To catch my attention
She walked with purpose
Her voice so soft
I had to lean in to hear her
My hand brushed her
Her skin soft and warm
Like stream water running across the sun warmed sand
To find the magic, to light those eyes with love
To find the magic to capture that heart as my own
To find the magic to make that smile a laugh
These are my 3 wishes
No riches no power no fame would equal this woman's love

Fickle heart
Should you seek to win her heart
You must show some of yourself
And do not depart from your true self
For if you show a false face you will lose that heart
Oh should you win
The contest has just begun
Now you must run to keep this love
Should you fall she will find another
Who will seek to win her heart
Once her heart has been lost
There will be no recapturing it

Her choice
She sits alone
When no one should be alone
Her choice
Her will
Is what is done
She sits alone
When she needs company
Her choice
Her will
Is what is done
She hides her sadness
By ignoring her loneliness
Her choice
Her will
Is what is done
The light tries to shine in her night
She says no to him it is her right
Her choice
Her will
Is what is done
Where will her happiness come from
By a man's hands or her emerging from the dark
Or will God intervene and offer his loving light.
Or will she remain in the night alone
Her choice
Her will
 Is what is done

Lost Hope
My love will always be yours to have
Your love will was never meant for me to have
My body yearns for your touch
My heart to hear you voice
My soul for the love that will never be mine
I cannot fault as I began a love affair
That should never have been
I captured your interest not your heart
My love will always be yours to have
Your love was never meant for me to have

I don't know who I seek
I don't know who I seek
I thought I know what it was I wanted
 I know who it was I wanted
It was not to be for me
It was not to be for her
It seemed so clear to me at the time
We were meant to be for all time
But now that's not true
But what is to be is so unclear
I don't know who I seek
Do you

Her name was not Aryanne
She owns the music she dances to
The crowd senses her within
The band sees not the crowd
 But the woman with the
Dark hair blowing in the wind
She journeys at her own pace
 She travel s as far as she wishes
She stands on the edge of a cliff
 Dark hair blowing in the wind
Her friends think they know her
Her family depends on her
But she is her own
Dark hair blowing in the wind
I commented to catch her attention
But many have sought that attention
Many have vied for the heart
 Of the woman with the
Dark hair blowing in the wind
Who captures that heart
It is not a heart to be won
But a heart that will be given
By the woman with the
Dark hair blowing in the wind

Here's to bad judgement
It's a bitch being alone
It's a bitch being so fucking alone
It's a bad combination lonely and horny
Bad judgment is just on the tip of my tongue
Focuses on a good girl see if you can get her attention
 I can wait for her to trust me, to sleep with her
I can be true to her if she sleeps with me
But being alone and horny leads to bad judgment
So let's not wait too long sweetheart before you take the plunge
The sooner the better for us both, less complicated

One of a kind
When the sun rises in the morn
It gets its sparkle from her smile
When the gentle breeze crosses the water
She has laughed
When the sprinkle of spring rain falls
She is sad
When a storm brews off the coast
She is unhappy
She is the only woman of her kind
Many a man has sought to capture this woman's heart
Many a man has failed
Many more will fail before the day is done
The heart she seeks has been allusive
The clues as to his where bouts hidden within
Is he who she thinks he is or is he within her grasp
Only to be passed for the illusion of whom she seeks
Her truth like her happiness lies within her own heart
 She seeks the only man of her kind
She is the only woman of her kind
Like us all who seek that one of our kind
We will seek until we find
Or God gives us peace

All about the Spark
A spark in one heart falls on stone
A spark in two hearts falls on dry leaves
A fire in one heart smothers for lack of the other
A fire in two hearts cannot be contained
The passion of one is soon lost or becomes greedy
The passion of two fuels one another
I pray God that my spark finds another
Let my fire burn freely
Let my passion fuel another
Let me know true love before I die

On a walk
Once while walking on a sunny path
I happened upon a red rose
Such was the beauty of this rose
That I built a house next to it
I tilled a garden around it
And for the rest of my days
I live in peace with the red rose
Always in sight and within my grasp

Love never discovered
I can see her in my mind
But where is she in the real world
I hear her voice inside my ears
But have never heard her speak
I feel her hands on my body
Yet never been near her
Can feel her passion building
Never have I touched her
The older I get
The further away she seems to be
As I lay on my death bed
I don't see nor hear nor feel her at all
Maybe after death she will be there already
Waiting for me

Later…not
So I spotted you online
It was a snowy day
And I wanted to be outside
But to damn cold
You are so pretty and
Your profile is so smart
I commented and invited you to chat
You ignored me, I tried to be clever
And pleasant
This is who I am
You continued to ignore me
I said goodbye and wished you well
It's not just that you could have been
The one I seek
But I may have been the one
You are still seeking
So easy to pass by
So easy to pass judgment
So easy to miss the one
That you will now never find

Another Spring?

The cold and wet makes my bones feel damp
The chill makes my legs so stiff
The cold wind makes my heart ache
I know that spring is not far away
I yearn for the warmth that will come
My legs need to be flexed
My heart needs to heal
Here comes spring how will I deal
With the thawing of my feelings
The drying of my bones and my tears
Will spring bring new love
Or has that moment passed me by
If so then no springs or summers left for me
Only fall and winters remain
Oh Lord let me know another spring before I die
Let me know that feeling of warmth in my heart and soul
Let me know that closeness I have missed so these past years
Let me have communion with another
Oh Lord let me know another spring before I die

Church Lady
She wonders why she is alone
She goes to church but all are too young
Or too old
She smiles everywhere she goes
But no one wants to kiss those smiling lips
She has an idea of who she wants
She wants the man her dad was
She wants a man that has no flaws
That never cries or has pain or feels down
Always strong as though not human
She grieves of the downfall o f men who
Feel pain and will weep at the pain of others
Who know what the bottom of life feels like
She does not realize her father's pain
His depression that he could never show
His desire to let it go but never the release he desired
How much happier he would have been
To have been a person instead of an image
That no one could live and be happy with
So she wonders why she is alone
She wants the man her dad was
She will hunt far and wide and maybe one day
She will find a man that her dad was
Until then she smiles everywhere she goes
And wonders why she is so alone

The Light in your eyes
I see the light in your eyes
I want to see my reflection in those eyes
I see the sun has touched your skin
I want to caress your skin
I see the smile on your lips
But all I can think of is kissing those lips

Pretty Girl in the Store
I am walking through the store
Not a care in the world
I see you down the isle
Picking out your island soap
You're so cute you're so hot
You're so innocent and so not
What do I say and still stay cool
I don't want to get slapped
Or arrested or laughed at
If I had your number I would text you
Let's go out to dinner
If I had your email I would email you
And ask you out to coffee
If I knew your kirk or your instagram
Or maybe your tweet
 I would if I could
Tell you of my new found love
For you
Pretty girl in the store

Lost you
I can see you moving across the field
Of people
If I blink I will lose you in the throng
Of people
Around the corner you go lost in a crowd
Of people
There a reflection on the glass across from the group
Of people
Gone never to be found again in the mass
Of people

I don't know maybe I am wrong but can there be love without coffee?

Coffee
Coffee what a blessing you are
Coffee you taste as luxury would taste
Coffee you make me feel alive when I wish I was not
Coffee you make me feel awake though I am not
Coffee your aroma makes me want to wake even earlier
Coffee you make me so happy
Coffee make me laugh but please don't spill on my white shirt
Even cold you make me smile at my stained shirt

Sleep Good
Sleep good sleep tight
My sweet heart so lost to me tonight
Don't stir don't toss
Just relax and let your dreams carry you off
I will dream of not being alone any longer
Of being with you on a sunny warm day
Sitting by the garden you working on a puzzle
Me working on a poem or a song
Or maybe we work on a song together
I do the words you do the music
But for tonight
Sleep good sleep tight tonight
My sweet heart so lost to me
Don't stir don't toss
Just relax and let your dreams carry you off
As the summer wind will carry you south

Night Life in a Boring Town
I move through the streets in the dark
It's a small town and no one is out
Though early on a Saturday night
Many houses are darkened
The only noises are when a train passes
Off in the distance or a one of the few cars
Pass by on the main highway a couple blocks away
As I move down the street I can on occasion
Hear a dog barking behind me
Approaching the down town the dark is broken
With street lights and business signs
Sounds of cars and people begin to filter through the silence
Still a small town but here there are three bars and a
restaurant
Here are the young folks that have not gone across the river
To the bigger town, here the couples out for an evening
A group of singles here and there to top off the mix
And well me

Lonely Tonight
Sitting up late
No one to date
So bored and lonely
To go for a walk
Holding hands
Laughing out loud
Would love to make out
To be touched by someone
To run my hands across
A woman's cheek
To lean in close
And whisper in her ear
To look up and see a tear
Of joy in her eye
Never to say good bye

Searching for you is a labor of love
Searching for you in the bars
Watching for you in the isles
When I am out walking I look for you
While getting my gas I keep my eyes open for you
I search the dating sites for you
My eyes are always roaming the streets while driving
I hope to meet you when I order my food
I thought I had met you at the reception desk
And almost had you at the cashiers station
But as hard as it is to look for you
Finding you is even harder

D&K
He had to travel across the world to find her
Didn't know he was looking for her
But he was
He knew it was special when he awoke on her floor one morning
To her mother fixing breakfast
There is something going on here
Not sure what exactly it is
But there is something going on here
And it's time to sort it out
When he did understand it was love
But now what
That they were to be together was easy
That they actually stay together was not so easy
So many a bump and many a lump
Was felt in the road of life and love
But when her eye fell on him no matter the mood
The love sprung forward as sharp and deadly as any weapon
When she was out of his reach the memory of that look of love
Would drive him out of his mind with desire and yearning
And soon no bumps or lumps became big enough
To cost them this love
So now they go forward many a challenge ahead
But never will this love be derailed
And the look they give each other speaks to the truth
As their love springs forward as sharp and deadly as any two weapons

Shake that booty
Know where to go when the big quake shakes
You go to the dance floor
Shake your booty back and forth
You shake your booty up and down
Do the quake baby
Know where to go when the big quake shakes
Grab your baby and shake booty for as long as it takes
To make a bigger quake shake
Shake baby shake shake baby shake

What a cutie
What a cutie you are
What a sweetheart you seem to be
Even from far away
You make me want to sway to the music
Of a tropical band on a tropical beach
As I move closer I see you are far more than cute
I want to move close to you I want to say something
I want move close to you and brush against you
Just to be sure you are real
Oh my gosh she smiled at me
My heart is beating to fast will I have a heart attack
What should I say? Did I smile back? Is it too late to smile back?
Oh my God she is speaking to me…what did she say
She wants to know where I got my Fireball shirt
If only I could remember so make up something quick
If I'm sarcastic she will think me a dick
And that will end the moment that has just begun

The cycle
You were true and loving for too many years
You put up with sarcasm, you put up with the laziness
You touched yourself more often than he touched you
Then one day after the kids moved out
He says there is someone else that meets his needs
We have grown apart he says as he packs his bag
You go through the motions, you get an attorney
You fill out the forms, you do the deposition
And now you are divorced
You go out with your friends you take up golf and Kayaking
 You consider skydiving
And after a while a year goes by and then another
Then its five, you have never really paid attention
To the attention that was given you
By men you hardly knew
But then one day you realize that something is missing
A companion that you never really had
The attention of someone who cares for you
The laughter shared
The mundane for one that is an adventure for two
Knowing you can be silly or passionate without being judged
Now the hunt is on
You evaluate your friends your coworkers
You have a different attitude when flirted with
Online dating, singles events
Somewhere someone will be the one

So many loves on my mind
So many loves on my mind
So many women want me to mind
Heather wants to tether me to her oasis
Sue wants to glue me to her side
Me I just want to see them both
When I need their brand love

So many loves on my mind
So many women want me to mind
Kristie wants me to be her Christian husband
Kathleen wants me to eat ice cream from her cone
Me I just want to see them both
When I need their brand love

So many loves on my mind
So many women want me to mind
Julie wants to tie herself to my pole
Sally May what me to be the mole in her hole
Me I just want to see them both
When I need their brand love

So many women so little time
So much fun don't bother to pine
Lose one today gain two tomorrow
So many loves on my mind
So many women what me to mind

Surfing on Mercer Island
Surfen surfen surfen riding the surf
Rideing the Mercer surfing circuit
Surfen surfen surfen riding the Mercer surf
Watching for the Mercer Island surfing queen
The waters cold and the surf is small
Damn few surf it at all
But there on the horizon you see you know
Is the Mercer Island surfing queen
Surfen surfen surfen riding the surf
Rideing the Mercer surfing circuit
Surfen surfen surfen riding the Mercer surf
Watching for the Mercer Island surfing queen
Now here she is catching a wave
She's the Mercer Island surfing queen
She doesn't hang ten with her toes
She rides her board on her head
As the Mercer Island people know
Surfen surfen surfen riding the surf
Rideing the Mercer surfing circuit
Surfen surfen surfen riding the Mercer surf
Watching for the Mercer Island surfing queen
Her fingers gripping
Her head is slipping
But she hangs ten fingers going into the bend
She's the Mercer Island surfing queen

Sitting on the edge
I discovered you sitting on the edge of a ledge
On a planter
What nice little smile on your cute little face
The pace of my heart quickened a bit
Could this be the one
So hard to tell from a photo and a few words
So easy to fill in the blanks when you have lived this long
The story is short but has the hint of hurt been done
So easy to fill in the blanks when you have lived this long
I reached out and said hello
We chatted a bit but the distance is clear
As you held you arm out to keep me back
You did not reject but held back to be friends
Could this be the one
So easy to fill in the blanks when you have lived this long
A lesson learned long ago
Many can still the body and occupy the mind
Few can touch your soul
It is better to be friends with someone special
Than to miss that opportunity to have your soul touched
Even from a distance and so I accept the conditions
But still life rolls along and the question lingers
Could this be the one
No matter how long you have lived life is still a mystery
I thank God for my life and for the mystery

Loving the morning
It's a beautiful morning
It's a lovely day
I think I'm going stay here
At least for a spell
Don't know which way I'll go today
But it won't be far
It's a beautiful morning
It's a lovely day
Who knows who I'll meet today
Maybe she'll be lovely as the day today
Maybe she'll have to smile when I sing her this song
Maybe she'll laugh when I ask her name
It's a beautiful morning
It's a lovely day
Maybe we'll have lunch today
Maybe later we'll have dinner
Maybe a glass of wine afterwards
Maybe we'll have pancakes in the morning
It's a beautiful morning
It's a lovely day
I think I like this place better
Every day that goes by
Every morning I meet someone new
Every day I'm here is a new day
It's a beautiful morning
It's a lovely day

White Salmon
I came here to heal
And heal I shall
In the crisp winter air
Overlooking the Columbia River
Under the watch of Mount Hood
Here in White Salmon
I came here to heal
And heal I shall
My soul will have the scars
My face the added lines
But my mind will be right
My goals changed but goals I will have
I came here to heal
And healing I am
Here in White Salmon
Spring will be here before long
The air will begin to warm
The sun will shine again
I will be healed by then
Here in White Salmon
I will make my home

White Salmon is one of my favorites but this next one gave me great joy to write and to this day one of my favorites.

Sing Loudly Dance Wildly
I can't sing worth a damn
But I sing as often as I can
I sing to the radio
I sing with the online music
I sing so softly when others might hear
I sing so loudly when I don't care
I sing to my dogs
They don't sing with me
I sing myself to sleep at night
I wake with a song on my lips
I sing in my truck
To songs I make up
And like this song they may not be good
But I sing them anyway for my own good
I can't dance worth a damn
Oh my God I dance all I can
I dance to the radio
I dance to the online music
I dance so low and slow when others might see
I dance so high and fast when I don't care who sees
I dance with my dogs
They dance with me
I dance when falling asleep at night
I'm dance when I awake in the morn
I dance in my truck
To songs I make up
And like this song and dance they may not be good
But I sing and dance for my own good

About the Author.
First let me just say what a cool guy he is and oh my God good looking as well. I did own a bar for several years with a now x wife. Before that I worked in the corporate world. I only began writing poems and lyrics a few months ago and have never published anything in my life until now and I am sure that it shows.
If we meet somewhere please, do not ask me to recite any of my works, as after they are written most of them no longer reside in my brain. I constantly have something new being cooked in my head. I hope you have enjoyed reading this book. I have become driven to write and to publish.
It is my goal that you find something in this book or any of my future books that will leave you with thoughts or feelings you did not start the day with.
Oh yes I am single so.
I would love to love you if only but a night
But please let's not talk of any spite
Only of the love that feels so right
Tonight

d.hooker@yahoo.com
https://www.facebook.com/don.hooker.7330

If you are interested in using any of my poems or lyrics to perform or record as part of your musical endeavors please contact me directly. I am also available to write or co write lyrics for commercial use.

Made in the USA
Middletown, DE
07 September 2020